Pennies

Written by Suzanne Lieurance
Illustrated by Tom Payne

Children's Press®
A Division of Scholastic Inc.
New York • Toronto • London • Auckland • Sydney
Mexico City • New Delhi • Hong Kong
Danbury, Connecticut

For my parents, Mary Ann and Denson Smith, with love
—S.L.

Reading Consultants

Linda Cornwell
Literacy Specialist

Katharine A. Kane
Education Consultant
(Retired, San Diego County Office of Education
and San Diego State University)

Library of Congress Cataloging-in-Publication Data
Lieurance, Suzanne.
 Pennies / written by Suzanne Lieurance ; illustrated by Tom Payne.
   p. cm. — (Rookie reader)
 Summary: A child needs one more penny to make a nickel.
  ISBN 0-516-22286-4 (lib. bdg.)   0-516-27818-5 (pbk)
  [1. Coins—Fiction. 2. Counting—Fiction. 3. Stories in rhyme.] I. Payne, Thomas, ill.
 II.Title. III. Series.
  PZ8.3.L598 Pe 2002
  [E] —dc21
                                    2001008489

3

I spent one penny.

5

 = 1¢

6

before one got spent.

A penny is one cent.

I had five pennies

12

I need a nickel.

A nickel is five cents.

How much do
I need if one penny
has been spent?

One penny,
two pennies,
three pennies, four.

Five make
a nickel, so . . .

I want one more.

Hmm . . . one penny, two pennies, three pennies, four.

A nickel is
five pennies.
Look . . .

I found one more!

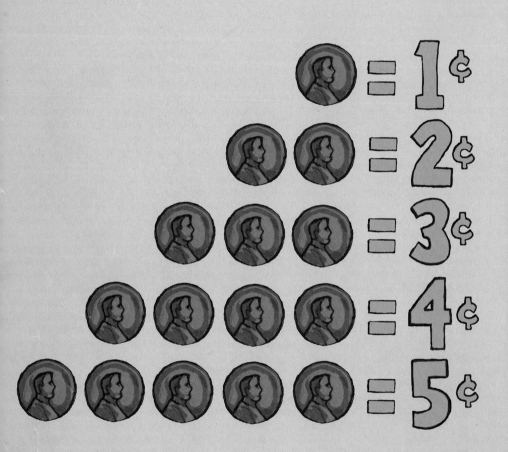

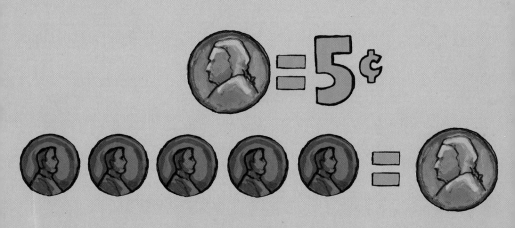

Word List (31 words)

a	has	nickel
been	hmm	one
before	how	pennies
cent	I	penny
cents	if	so
do	is	spent
five	look	three
found	make	two
four	more	want
got	much	
had	need	

About the Author

Suzanne Lieurance counts her pennies from her home in Kansas City, Missouri, where she lives with her husband, two sons, and three dogs. Her other books include *Kidding around Kansas City, School Projects for Pennies, The Space Shuttle Challenger Disaster, A Child's First Pet,* and *Shoelaces* (another Rookie Reader). Suzanne is also an instructor for the Institute of Children's Literature in West Redding, Connecticut.

About the Illustrator

Tom Payne has been a humorous illustrator for a very long time. His work has appeared in all sorts of books and magazines. He commutes into his studio, which he shares with some other "arty" people, in Albany, New York, from his home in the nearby Helderberg Mountains. He lives with his wife, Anne, and his sons, Thomas and Matthew.